MW01153988

No Longer Property of
ANYTHINK LIBRARIES/
RANGEVIEW LIBRARY DISTRICT

NO LONGER PROPERTY OF
ANYTHINK LIBRARIES
RANGEVIEW LIBRARY DISTRICT

ENERGY EVOLUTIONS

SOLAR POWER

Robyn Hardyman

CHERITON
CHILDREN'S BOOKS

Please visit our website, www.cheritonchildrensbooks.com to see more of our high-quality books.

First Edition

Published in 2022 by **Cheriton Children's Books**
PO Box 7258, Bridgnorth WV16 9ET, UK

© 2022 Cheriton Children's Books

Author: Robyn Hardyman
Designer: Paul Myerscough
Editor: Victoria Garrard
Proofreader: Wendy Scavuzzo
Picture Researcher: Rachel Blount
Consultant: David Hawksett, BSc

Picture credits: Cover: Shutterstock/Think4photop; Inside: p1: Shutterstock/Lukassek; p3: Shutterstock/Rudmer Zwerver; p4: Shutterstock/Xfox01; p5: Shutterstock/Oliveromg; p6: Shutterstock/Luiggi33: p7: Shutterstock/Baciu; p8: Shutterstock/Neijia; p9: Shutterstock/Elena Elisseeva; p10: Shutterstock/Graphixmania; p11: Shutterstock/Jeff Whyte; p12: Shutterstock/Cup Of Spring; p13: Wikimedia Commons/Raysonho @ Open Grid Scheduler/Grid Engine; p14: Shutterstock/Pittha Poonotoke; p15: Shutterstock/ Smallcreative; p16: Shutterstock/Lukassek; p17: Shutterstock/Droneandy; p18: Shutterstock/Rudmer Zwerver; p19: Shutterstock/Thaweesak Thipphamon; p20-21: Shutterstock/Piotr Zajda; p21: Shutterstock/John Andrus; p22: Shutterstock/ArtisticPhoto; p23: Shuttestock/Dominic Dudley; p24: Shutterstock/Simone Hogan; p25: Shutterstock/ You Touch Pix of EuToch; p26: Shutterstock/Adriana Mahdalova; p27: Shutterstock/ lcswart; p28: Stanford University/Jin Xie; p29: Shutterstock/Valeriya Anufriyeva; p30: Shutterstock/Abriendomundo; p31: Renovagen Ltd; p32: Flickr/ Stephan Ridgway; p33: Shutterstock/Timofeev Vladimir; p34: Shutterstock/Photolike; p35: Shutterstock/ Iaremenko Sergii; p36: Shutterstock/KrimKate; p37: Oxford PV; p38: Shutterstock/Jochen Netzker; p39: Shutterstock/Reinhard Tiburzy; p40: © SonoMotors; p41: Shutterstock/Igor Karasi; p42: Shutterstock/Jayk67; p43: Shutterstock/Dreamnikon; p44: Shutterstock/ Sean Pavone; p45: Shutterstock/Smileus.

All rights reserved. No part of this book may be reproduced in any form without permission from the publisher, except by reviewer.

Printed in the United States of America

Contents

CHAPTER 1

What Is Solar Power?

The sun is a star. It's a huge ball of super-hot gas that is powered by nuclear reactions in its core. This giant produces masses of energy. Scientists have found ways to use some of this energy to meet our need for power. This is solar power, and it is the world's fastest-growing source of energy.

Cleaner Energy

More than half of the energy the world uses comes from burning coal, oil, and natural gas in **power plants**. Coal, oil, and natural gas are **fossil fuels**. They are in limited supply, so these energy sources are called **nonrenewable**. It took millions of years for fossil fuels to form, so we cannot replace them. Burning fossil fuels to make electricity creates harmful gases that are trapping more heat from the sun and warming our **atmosphere**. This is causing changes to the global **climate**, which can have catastrophic effects on our planet.

The sun is a **renewable** energy source. Unlike fossil fuels, it will not run out.

Scientists are warning us that we need to reduce our use of fossil fuels and instead try to use renewable forms of energy, such as solar power from the sun. The sun is an energy source that produces no harmful **emissions**, because nothing is burned. Solar power simply transforms sunlight into energy.

The Sun's Energy

The sun is 93 million miles (150 million km) away. Yet every hour, enough energy from the sun reaches Earth to meet the whole world's energy needs for a year. What is more, it takes that energy just eight minutes to get here! The sun gives us light and heat, and these are what make life on Earth possible. Plants make food from sunlight, and animals eat plants. For thousands of years, people have been using the sun's light and heat. We have grown our crops in sunlight and concentrated the sun's rays to light fires. Now we are finding even better ways to capture that energy to power our world.

BIG Issues
Energy All the Time

The world's population is growing fast, and in the big developing nations, such as India, more people can afford the things that use electricity. These include heating and cooling systems, and all the machines of modern life. The **rural** areas of developing countries, however, often do not have a reliable electricity **grid** delivering power to every home. One solution is solar power, which can provide energy on a small scale or a huge scale. A solar power **installation** on a single building can give it **off-grid** power any time the sun shines.

The sun gives us light and heat, and makes life on Earth possible. Its energy feeds the plants that feed other living things, including us, to give them energy.

Thermal Solar Power

Solar power uses the energy of the sun in one of two forms—heat energy or light energy. Of the two, light energy is most widely used to generate **electricity, and this is what is transforming energy industries around the world. There is also an important role for heat energy, however. It can be used in countries with warm climates to provide heat and electricity where no other type of energy may be available.**

Heated by the Sun

Using the heat of the sun is called **thermal solar power, or concentrated solar power (CSP). In countries with warm, sunny climates, the sun's heat is used directly to heat water. A solar water heater, called a collector, is installed on the roof of a building to catch the sun. Flat plate collectors are the most common type used. Under their glass cover is a network of tubes filled with liquid that heats up in the sun and, in turn, heats a container of water. The heated water is pumped to a storage tank, which can be inside or outside the building.

Thermal solar collectors can be used to heat the water in an outdoor swimming pool. They can easily heat the water to 75 to 85 degrees Fahrenheit (24 to 29 °C).

By using a solar water heater or a solar oven, people who live in places without electricity can still heat their water or cook food.

Safer Cooking

Solar heating can also be used for cooking. Millions of people around the world do not have electricity and cook over fires that are fueled by wood or animal waste. The smoke from these fuels is bad for people's health and also **pollutes** the atmosphere. Energy **innovators** have overcome this problem by creating solar ovens, so people can cook cleanly and for free. They can also boil water to make it safe to drink. A simple solar oven is a box surrounded by **reflective** panels. The panels direct the sunlight onto the food, which is placed in a closed cooking pot inside the box. The food is cut into small pieces to be cooked. The oven is put out in full sunshine, and cooking begins.

Working Despite Disaster

Another great advantage of solar ovens is that they are small and portable, or easy to move around. They can be set up anywhere in just a few minutes. This makes them ideal for areas that are difficult to reach or places that have been hit by a **natural disaster**. For example, if an earthquake has destroyed a region's electricity supply, solar ovens can be used to provide safe drinking water and hot food to people in need.

Electricity from Sunlight

Solar power makes electricity from sunlight using solar panels in a process called photovoltaics, or PV. People have been using this technology in a small way for many years in calculators and watches with small solar-powered batteries. But in the past 20 years, the energy industry has made this technology work for us on a huge scale. In recent years, the technology has become better and better, making solar power more efficient, flexible, and cheaper.

Super Silicon

In 1954, scientists discovered that a substance called silicon, which is found in sand, creates an **electric charge** when placed in plenty of sunlight. Soon after, chips were being made of silicon to power small devices. Today, solar panels are made of many **solar cells**. Each cell has several layers. The top layer is glass for protection. The next is a dark layer to keep the sunlight from reflecting off the glass. Under that are two thin wafers of silicon and metal wires. To make the wafers, the silicon is heated to a very high temperature. Chemicals are added to it that make **particles** in the silicon, called electrons, less tightly bonded to each other. When sunlight hits the silicon wafers, the electrons absorb some of the energy in it. This makes them start to move, and they flow along the metal wires. This movement of electrons is an electric current, or electricity.

Solar cells are made with silicon in very thin layers. Many cells are combined to make a single solar panel.

Installing solar panels on a roof is a skilled, specialized job. They must be handled very carefully.

Capturing Sunlight

PV cells are joined together to make panels, which are then installed on the roof of a building. The number of panels used depends on how much power is going to be needed in the building. The panels must be installed so they get as much sunlight as possible. In locations in the northern hemisphere (the area of Earth above an imaginary line around its center that we call the equator) this usually means putting them on a south-facing roof, tilted up at an angle. Excessive heat is not good for solar panels, however. It makes them perform poorly. A panel will produce more electricity on a sunny, cold day (especially if snow is reflecting the sunlight), than on a hot, clear day.

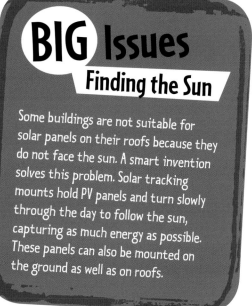

BIG Issues
Finding the Sun

Some buildings are not suitable for solar panels on their roofs because they do not face the sun. A smart invention solves this problem. Solar tracking mounts hold PV panels and turn slowly through the day to follow the sun, capturing as much energy as possible. These panels can also be mounted on the ground as well as on roofs.

CHAPTER 2

Solar Systems

The PV panels positioned on a roof are connected to a battery, which stores the electricity. Electricity can flow in two different forms, alternating current (AC) and direct current (DC). The electricity produced by the PV panels is DC, but we use AC electricity to power our homes because it is safer. In the solar power system, the electricity is converted, or changed, from DC to AC in a device called an inverter. This is located inside the home. From there, the electricity is directed to the fuse box. From the fuse box, the electricity is sent through wires throughout the home to supply lighting and power.

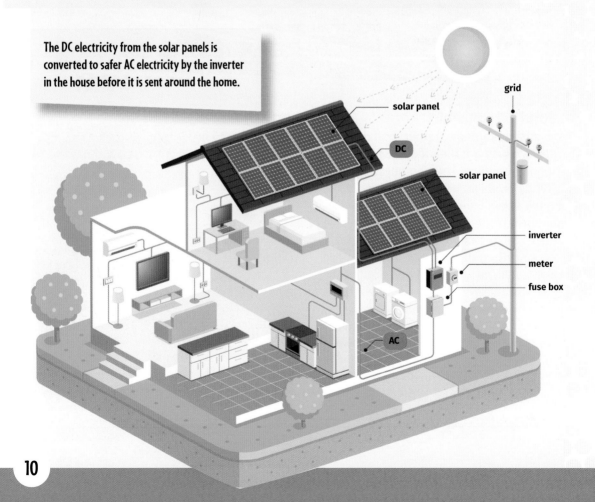

The DC electricity from the solar panels is converted to safer AC electricity by the inverter in the house before it is sent around the home.

grid

solar panel

DC

solar panel

inverter

meter

fuse box

AC

Simple and Easier

Inverters used to be large and expensive, so the start-up cost for installing solar power in a home was high. The industry has responded to this by developing microinverters. These are smaller and cheaper than inverters and a single microinverter can be connected to a single solar panel. That means customers can start small, even with just one PV panel, and build up their solar power system. The microinverters are also quick and easy to install. Experts think that the inverters will soon be built into the PV panels themselves, making the system even simpler and cheaper to install.

Good All-Around

Since 2009, the cost of installing solar power has fallen by about 60 percent. This is a result of several factors. The technology has improved in many ways, making the solar panels easier to install and more efficient at generating electricity. The number of people wanting solar power has increased hugely. With greater demand, the cost of making the panels and other equipment has fallen. According to the International Renewable Energy Agency (IRENA), there are more than 9 million people worldwide employed by the renewable energy industry. One of the fastest-growing jobs in the United States today is a solar PV installation technician. This growing industry is creating jobs, while also saving the **environment**.

PV panels can be installed on apartment buildings, too. In this example, they have a double purpose: to generate electricity for the building and to provide shade, keeping the inside cool.

A Regular Supply

You have set up your solar panels on the roof and, on a sunny day, they are generating a lot of electricity. Great! But what happens when the sun is not shining? If solar power is your main source of electricity, it is vital to have a regular power supply that you can rely on.

Sunshine or Cloud?

PV panels can produce electricity only when the sun is shining on them. When it shines directly onto them at noon, they work best and make a lot of electricity. When the sun is low in the sky or it is cloudy, less sunlight falls on them, and they do not work as well.

On a flat roof, PV panels can be angled to get the most sunlight possible.

In a sunny place such as southern California, there are about 5.5 hours of "usable" sunshine a day. The solution to providing a regular supply is to store the electricity in a battery. On sunny days, when more energy is produced than is needed, the battery stores the extra power for future use. The energy industry is working to improve the technology of these storage batteries, because they are vital to making solar power suitable for even more people. A battery also protects **consumers** from **power outages**. Solar power shuts down during a power outage, but a battery will automatically kick in and restore power.

Storing Power

In 2015, the American electric car company Tesla produced a rechargeable battery called Powerwall which became the most popular choice for residential use. In 2016, the Powerwall 2 was launched and, by early 2020, a total of 100,000 Powerwalls had been installed. Many companies are now putting a lot of research time and money into developing new and improved batteries for home energy storage. These include automotive companies, such as Mercedes-Benz and BMW, because electric cars need batteries that can store a lot of electricity, too. As more people switch to solar power and electric cars, this exciting technology will develop quickly.

BIG Issues

Can You Make Money from Solar?

With solar power installed in a building, the consumer will usually choose to connect the system to the grid, which is the main electricity network. If the solar panels are generating more electricity than the building needs, they may be able to send the excess back to the grid and be paid for it. This is called net metering, because the electricity meter shows whether the user is taking power from the grid or giving it back. If they are giving it back, the meter spins backward! Many states have allowed net metering to encourage people to change to renewable energy.

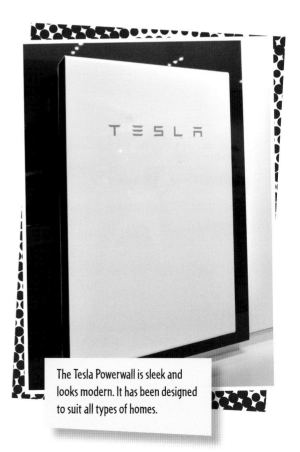

The Tesla Powerwall is sleek and looks modern. It has been designed to suit all types of homes.

Inside and Outside

Solar power is not just suitable for homes. Its great advantage is that it can be used on almost any scale, from a single PV cell to a massive array **of thousands of panels. There are many small-scale uses of solar energy that are transforming the way we power our outdoor spaces.**

Solar Streets

Many people install a few solar lights in their backyard to use the day's sunshine to make their garden look attractive after dark and to provide light. This technology is increasingly being used in public places for important functions such as street lighting. A few PV panels above each light give it the power it needs to run through the night. Signs along the road are often powered by solar panels, too. Some cities, such as San Diego, California, are using solar streetlights in more complex ways. The Smart City San Diego Initiative is incorporating smart **sensors** into streetlights. These can direct drivers to open parking spaces and help first responders during emergencies. Combining Internet-linked sensors with solar-powered streetlights saves time and money.

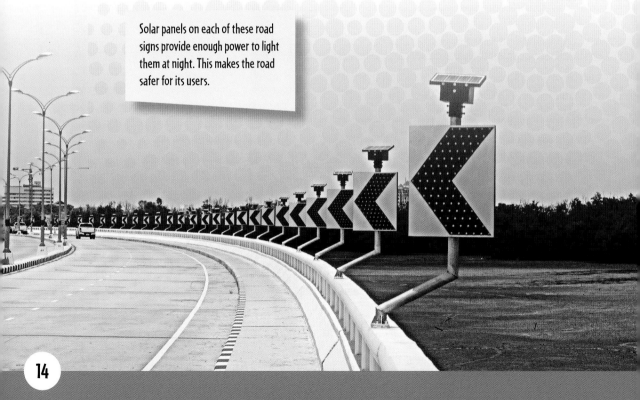

Solar panels on each of these road signs provide enough power to light them at night. This makes the road safer for its users.

These carports provide shade for the vehicles, while also generating electricity to power the business.

The sidewalks along interstate highway Route 66 have been chosen to test another exciting new solar idea—a solar-powered road. Imagine a roadway that can generate its own electricity and use it to power not only road signs and lights, but also the electric cars driving along it. Light bulbs in the road surface could light the route at night, and heating elements in it could melt snow and ice in winter. There are a few problems with the idea, however. The panels cannot be tilted toward the sun, and when there are cars driving over them, they are in shade. The idea would certainly be better suited to roads in sunny, open country, with light traffic flow, than to the busy city streets of a town or city.

Making Money and Keeping Cool

In sunny places, people often seek shade to keep cool. Solar panels can be the perfect solution to meeting this need. Companies in sunny locations need to provide parking lots for their workers. These need to be shady to keep the cars cool through the day. What better way to provide shaded parking than with raised solar panels that can generate electricity for the business at the same time? AVX Corporation in South Carolina, for example, is a manufacturer of electronic components that employs 1,000 people. In 2019, it unveiled a new 10-canopy system in the employee parking lot, which provides clean, **sustainable** energy and plenty of shaded parking spaces.

CHAPTER 3

Solar for All

Hundreds of thousands of consumers are installing solar power in their homes and businesses, so they can generate their own electricity from a clean, renewable source. That is not possible for everyone, however, and to make a big difference to the way that countries generate their power, solar power needs to be used on a massive scale in solar power plants. That clean electricity can then be provided in the normal way, through the grid, so everyone can benefit from it.

Space and Sunshine

Solar power plants need large areas of land. Hundreds or even thousands of PV panels are laid out across the land, tilted toward the sun. They do not produce any pollution, but they stand out on the landscape, which is why the largest power plants are often located in faraway areas. The panels are all connected to a central hub where the electricity collects to be distributed. To maximize the amount of energy the panels can extract from the sunlight, panels are

This huge solar power plant in Germany covers a wide area of the landscape.

sometimes mounted on trackers rather than being fixed at a particular tilt. The latest trackers allow the panels to follow the daily path of the sun. They are more expensive than standard installation systems. However, they soon pay for themselves, because they can increase the amount of electricity produced by up to 20 percent.

Kamuthi Solar Park

The biggest solar power plants are enormous. In India, for example, the Kamuthi solar park in Tamil Nadu covers 2,500 acres (1,012 ha) and consists of 2.5 million solar panels. This site is expected to generate enough electricity for 750,000 people. It is cleaned every day by a robotic system, which is powered by its own solar panels.

BIG Issues
Changing Minds

One of the big challenges in achieving the shift from generating electricity from fossil fuels to cleaner sources, such as solar, is that people become stuck in their ways. Most people are used to not thinking too hard about where their power comes from. Gradually, we are learning that we need to care about it. That process can be helped by good examples being set by some of the big players, and this is starting to happen. Big companies, for example, are starting to buy their electricity directly from the owners of large solar parks. This is good business for them, but it also sends a message to everyone that **clean energy** is the way of the future.

The giant tech companies in the United States are buying their energy from renewable sources. For example, Apple's headquarters is powered by 100 percent renewable energy, in part from a massive rooftop solar installation.

Keeping It Local

The massive solar power plants being built around the world today have an important purpose: to generate electricity for people across a wide area. Alongside these impressive projects, however, other innovators are developing solar power that operates on a different scale.

Sunshine Gardens

A few years ago, an innovator named David Amster-Olszewski in Colorado Springs, Colorado, had an idea. He realized that many people in his neighborhood would like to use solar power, but were unable to install it in their own homes. Perhaps their apartment building was not suitable, or they rented their home instead of owning it. He started a company called SunShare to help people.

SunShare sets up community solar "gardens." These are solar power operations on a scale bigger than a single house, but much smaller than a standard **commercial power plant**. People in a neighborhood buy shares in a handful of local panels set up by SunShare, and are connected to its electricity supply. Money is taken off their regular utility bill based on how much electricity they get from the solar panels.

Community solar projects like this one give people access to clean solar power without having to install solar panels on their own property.

Powered Up

This smart idea has caught on, and there are now thousands of similar projects, each serving a few hundred households in communities across the United States and in other countries. In New York State, for example, a project called NY-Sun runs access to hundreds of community solar installations across the state. Customers find a provider close to where they live and pay for the plan that works best for them. There are no upfront costs, and plans can last for as long as needed.

Finding Solutions

In some countries where the population is high and the land is crowded, it can be difficult to find the space required for generating solar power. Japan, which is made up of four main islands and many small ones, is one such country. Even there, however, the power industry has found a way to make space for solar power, by installing floating solar panels on lakes and **reservoirs**. These "floatovoltaics" bring extra benefits, too. The cooling effect of the water improves the performance of the PV panels, and the installation reduces the amount of water that **evaporates** from the lake or reservoir. This is great idea for **drought**-prone areas, and it is now being used in the United States, India, Brazil, and elsewhere.

Putting solar panels on lakes is a good option when land is overcrowded or unsuitable.

Scaling Up Solar Power

We have seen that CSP, using the heat of the sun rather than its light, is widely used in hot countries to heat water for homes and public facilities, such as swimming pools. Over the past 10 years, it has also taken off on a much bigger scale as huge thermal power plants have been built to generate electricity for the grid.

Focus the Heat

There are two main types of solar thermal power plants. The first collects the sun's energy using rows and rows of long, rectangular curved mirrors. These mirrors focus sunlight onto tubes that run down their length, heating up the fluid inside them. The hot fluid is sent to a central location where it is used to boil water, which creates steam that drives a **generator** to produce electricity. The mirrors tilt with the sun, to keep sunlight focused on the tubes throughout the day. There are several plants with this design operating in the Mojave Desert in California today.

The second design is newer. This also uses a large field of mirrors, called heliostats, but they are flat. They can track the sun through the day, but they also reflect and concentrate the sunlight onto the top of a tower in the center of the field.

The Ivanpah Solar Electric Generating System was built on 6 square miles (16 square km) of public land in the Mojave Desert in California.

The sunlight can be made 1,500 times more powerful with this method. Inside the tower, the intense heat is used to heat water to make steam that runs the generator in the same way. Industry experts are experimenting with using different chemicals that can hold their heat for longer than water can.

Ganging Up

Each heliostat usually stands on its own, with two mirrors and a motor to help track the sun. But a company is looking at an alternative to combine those heliostats and save money. They call the approach "ganged" heliostats, a format that allows more mirrors to share the same motor and stand. This approach could cut the cost of installing heliostats by half.

In 2013, the biggest CSP plant in the world opened at Ivanpah, in the Mojave Desert. There, three massive towers are surrounded by more than 170,000 heliostats, and enough electricity is produced to power up to 140,000 homes.

BIG Issues
Harming Wildlife

Huge thermal power plants need a lot of space, and their intense heat can be harmful to local wildlife. Construction at Ivanpah was scaled back from its original design because of its suspected impact on the local desert tortoise.

Developers of solar farms need to take notice of their impact on the environment, including any hazard they may pose to the local wildlife.

CHAPTER 4

Where in the World?

The sun shines everywhere in the world for some of the time, even though some countries are hotter than others. Generating electricity using PV panels does not need the sun's heat, only its light, so it can potentially be used almost anywhere. Over the past decade, the solar power industry has grown enormously, as countries around the world realize the importance of switching to clean energy.

Signing Up to Change

In 2015, 194 countries plus the 28 countries of the European Union (EU) agreed to sign the Paris Agreement, an agreement within the United Nations (UN) Framework Convention on **Climate Change**. Under the Paris Agreement, each country must set targets for reducing its level of harmful emissions. The United States left the Agreement under President Trump but has rejoined it under President Biden.

The binding targets are encouraging countries to develop renewable energy, including solar power. At the moment, the biggest solar power generators are the United States and China. Together, they make up two-thirds of the global growth in solar power. However, there are always new projects being planned, so the list of the biggest producers is always changing. In 2017, about 35 percent of the newly installed power capacity across the world came from PV panels, making it an even bigger energy provider than wind power.

This waterfront in the Chinese city of Shanghai is covered in solar panels to provide power to the city.

In the Middle East, the Mohammed bin Rashid Al Maktoum Solar Park in Dubai is currently being built and already covers a large area of desert. It will generate electricity for local homes and businesses.

China, Leading the Way

China has more solar-energy capacity than any other country in the world. It has created several very large power plants, such as the Longyangxia Dam facility in Tibet, which has a staggering 4 million PV panels. One of the largest plants in the world today is also in China, in the Tengger Desert. China is also the biggest manufacturer of solar PV cells and panels, followed by Taiwan and Malaysia. Chinese companies are also developing solar power in other countries, such as Hungary and Poland.

The Middle East and India

The countries of the Middle East may be the big oil suppliers of the world, but now they are looking to make the most of their high levels of sunshine by creating power for themselves. India has three of the world's biggest solar plants. In 2019, the government approved a plan that is worth around $1.2 billion to support growth in the industry, using government-owned companies. All the PV cells and panels must be made in India, and all the power will be used by the government.

The United States

In 2017, solar power provided less than 2 percent of the total electricity generated in the United States. However, the country is still a world leader in solar generation, creating about 15 percent of all the solar power globally. Solar is the country's third-largest renewable electricity source, after wind and hydroelectric **power**. There is a long way to go to develop this industry to its full potential, but businesses are working hard to make it happen.

Another Sunshine State

California leads the way in the solar power industry in the United States, with more than 15 percent of its power coming from solar energy in 2017. At the end of 2018, it became the first state to require solar panels to be installed on all new homes up to three stories high. The long-term energy bill savings for these households will be considerable, and they will be producing no harmful emissions. Thousands of homes in California already have solar panels installed.

California was the first state to require solar panels to be installed on all new condominium buildings.

One big growth area in solar power is small PV commercial plants that are producing enough electricity to feed into an energy-providing company. There are 2,500 of those in the United States, and almost 2,000 of them are small. Many are community solar projects, while others have been set up in response to help from local state authorities. This may include giving financial help, such as agreeing to pay a fixed price for the electricity over a long period of time.

Ready for Takeoff

The Energy Information Administration (EIA) estimates that the amount of solar power produced in power plants has tripled in just two years. They also think that the amount produced by small installations, such as on individual homes and businesses, has grown by more than 40 percent in the same period. These figures show how the solar power industry has geared up for expansion.

BIG Issues
Mixing It Up

Although solar power is expanding rapidly in the United States, the wind power industry is also growing rapidly. This is one of the big issues with renewables—no one power source can be enough to replace fossil fuels on its own. The future lies in having a combination of several different technologies, for solar and wind energy to join with hydroelectric, **geothermal**, and **biomass** energies, each of which can make a contribution. Together, they can build into a sustainable energy package for the twenty-first century.

This power plant in Palm Springs, California, has solar panels working alongside its wind power **turbines**.

Turning the Lights On

One of the great benefits of solar power is that it can be used on a small scale to deliver electricity to places where there is no power grid. In developing countries, such as many in Africa, there may be no network of cables carrying power to rural villages. People there rely on burning wood and other fuels for cooking, and candles or oil for lighting, along with battery-powered lamps. Nearly 20 percent of the world's population has no electricity, but innovations in solar power are now changing that.

People Changing Lives

Many of the projects bringing electricity to developing countries are small in scale. They are the work of innovative businesspeople or small groups that want to make change happen. For example, a few years ago, a group of college engineering students set up BBOXX. BBOXX is a company that delivers PV panels to homes in Rwanda in Africa. For their new panels, its customers pay a small amount—about the same as they were spending before on fuel.

Solar power is being used to power a flashlight, so this woman can work when the light is poor.

These houses on the edge of a city in South Africa all have solar thermal water-heating equipment on their roofs to give them hot water.

Many other innovators are doing similar work. Zola Electric, based in San Francisco, California, has taken solar power to 50,000 homes in Tanzania in Africa, and M-KOPA, a Kenyan company, has provided power to more than 500,000 homes in Kenya, Uganda, and Tanzania.

The effects of having solar power can transform lives. With electricity, for example, people can keep in touch with each other because they can charge a cell phone. They can stay up after dark, with lights that allow young people to study and improve their education. Having streetlights also makes communities safer.

Hot New Ideas

Developing countries in warm places also have another solar benefit. Their warm climate makes some of them suitable for thermal solar power. Recent research into the situation in India, Kenya, and Chile has found that there is a lot of potential for CSP there. The heat created on these plants would not necessarily be turned into electricity. Instead, it could be used directly, in local industries that use processes in which heat is needed. This could make it possible to set up valuable industries in areas not on the electricity grid. Some test projects are being set up to show that this technology can work and benefit a local area.

Changing Lives

Solar power can do so much more than just keep the lights on. The fact that it can be scaled down to a size that is portable makes off-grid solar power valuable in many ways that are bringing great benefits to the less-developed countries of the world.

Solar Power Is Saving Lives

Clean water is a most basic human need, but many people spend hours every day walking to find a safe supply of water for their families. This uses time that could be used for work or study. Dirty drinking water spreads diseases, but this is preventable. Researchers at Stanford University have discovered that sunlight can be used to clean dirty water. They have developed a tiny tablet that is simply dropped into dirty water. After a few minutes in sunlight, the water is clean and safe to drink. Solar power is also being used to make clean water from salty water. With supplies of fresh water under threat in some areas, this could save millions of lives.

This tiny tablet uses sunlight to clean dirty water in just a few minutes.

Keeping Things Cool

We take it for granted in our world that we can keep our food fresh for longer by storing it in a refrigerator. If you live off-grid, however, there is no electricity to power a refrigerator, television, or anything else. Cool drinks are great on a hot day, but sometimes refrigeration can make a difference to people's lives in a much more important way. For example, solar-powered refrigerators are now available that can allow farmers to store their fruit and vegetable crops for longer, so they do not have to sell them immediately after harvesting. They can sell them when the price is right.

A solar-powered refrigerator can also provide life-saving medical supplies. One of the best ways to improve the health of people in developing countries is to **vaccinate** them against the worst diseases.

Health programs send doctors and nurses to faraway areas with vaccines, but they must be kept cool to work. In these off-grid areas with no electricity supply, solar-powered portable refrigerators are making sure these essential vaccines can do their important work.

BIG Issues
The Need for Cooling

As countries in hot places develop and people there become wealthier, their need for air-conditioning units is growing. Energy experts think that soon the need for cooling in homes around the world will use even more energy than the need for heating. To deal with this issue, inventive solar industry engineers have created solar-powered air conditioners that can be run using either PV panels or thermal solar power.

Vaccines save millions of lives, but they must be kept cool to work properly. Solar-powered refrigeration makes this possible off-grid.

CHAPTER 5

New Ideas

Innovations in the technology of solar power are constantly transforming the industry, helping it take off as a major source of renewable energy. As solar power spreads across the world, these developments are making it cheaper to install solar power devices and making them better at changing sunlight into energy.

Double-Sided Panels

One innovative new way to get more power from solar PV panels is to make them so they can absorb sunlight on both sides. Standard panels have a metal backing, but these double-sided, or bifacial, panels remove most of that, exposing the PV cells to light on both sides. This design is more expensive to make and, until recently, it did not produce enough extra power to make that cost worthwhile. But now **manufacturing** costs have fallen. A double-sided panel does not produce twice as much power, because only one side can get the full force of the sunlight, but it can produce up to 25 percent more. It helps if the ground is painted white, so that more light bounces off the ground to hit the panel's underside.

Double-sided panels are especially well suited to cloudier locations, where the panel does not create deep shade on its underside.

Lasting for Longer

In the early days of solar power, the PV cells that were made tended to degrade, or wear down, after a few years. This made them less efficient at producing electricity. Today, solar panels can work efficiently from 25 to 40 years, depending on the manufacturer. Cheaper panels tend to degrade faster and not last as long, especially if they are positioned in places with harsh weather conditions or if they are not well maintained. Manufacturers are looking at all the factors that cause cracks to appear or joints to fail. They are also finding ways to change how each part is made, even down to the adhesives, or glues, used to make them last longer.

Solar for Emergencies

Solar power is the ideal energy source for emergency situations, such as after a natural disaster when power lines may be down and the rescue services urgently need electricity for their equipment. Solar panels are rigid and heavy, however, and easily damaged when moved. One innovator has come up with a really smart solution to this problem. Engineer John Hingley has created a flexible solar panel—a 0.3 inch (9 mm) thick PV sheet that rolls up like a carpet. It is called Rapid Roll, and it can be delivered by road or dropped in by helicopter to exactly where it is needed. Within a few minutes, it is ready to start generating electricity. John's company, Renovagen, has not stopped there. Their latest product is a Fast Fold Solar Mat, a smaller device that fits in the back of a car.

The Rapid Roll solar mat from Renovagen can be transported and unrolled wherever it is needed to provide electricity quickly.

Energy Storage

The key to the future success of solar energy is finding ways to store more of the power it generates, and for longer. Solar power plants may send power straight to the grid but, at very sunny times, they will generate more power than the grid needs. There needs to be a way to store that excess power for use when demand is high, but the sun is not shining.

Banks of batteries are needed to store excess electricity generated by a solar power plant in Australia. Altogether, there are 60 batteries.

Better Batteries

Some of the big players in the energy industry are investing a lot of money in new battery technology. Shell, for example, has bought an innovative German battery manufacturer and is investing in the company to help it work on improving the technology of their batteries for home users. These batteries give home consumers more control over managing the power their rooftop solar installations generate.

Storing the Sun

The solar power industry is also looking at all-new ways to store the sun's energy. One exciting new technology is to store that energy as heat, rather than electricity, and to store it in the form of a chemical. This is solar thermal fuel (STF). When the heat held by the fuel is needed, a small jolt of electricity or light is applied to the fuel to release it. Professor Jeffrey Grossman of Massachusetts Institute of Technology (MIT) and his team have been developing STFs in a solid rather than a liquid form. Their thin film material could be added to many other materials, such as glass or even fabric. It could be built into the glass of a car's windshield, for example. During the day, it would absorb heat from the sun and store it. It could then be triggered to release its heat after a cold night, when ice had formed on the windshield. The heat would melt the ice and clear the windshield. This could be very useful for electric cars, which use a lot of their battery power for deicing.

BIG Issues
Solar-Plus-Storage

The first solar power plants did not include any energy storage system, they just fed power into a grid. As solar power expands, the ability to store the power these plants produce has become essential. The industry is moving toward "solar-plus-storage," with battery storage built into the plants. This makes good financial sense, because the company can store the power and release it when the price is highest, at times of peak demand. Governments are buying into this advance, too. Several states, including California, Massachusetts, and New York, are setting targets for the amount of energy storage they want to see in the next few years.

Deicing the windshield in the morning may become a thing of the past if solid solar thermal fuels can be built into the glass.

Solar Buildings

Now that PV panels are becoming better at extracting the energy from sunlight, the industry is looking at new ways to install PV panels on our buildings. With this new technology, even more buildings can generate more solar-powered electricity.

In this new building, flexible solar panels have been designed to be part of the architecture.

A New Look for Solar Power

The falling price of PV panels has made solar power a more affordable option for many people to install on the roofs of their home. For some people, however, it is the look of solar panels rather than their cost that is keeping them from installing them.

The latest innovations can change all that. One company, Sistine Solar, has developed a thin film with built-in graphics, which is applied to the top of standard PV panels. The graphics can make the panels blend in with the rest of the roof in color and design, making them less visible.

Another business has gone one step further, with solar roof tiles that look exactly the same as standard shingles. The electric car giant, Tesla, is developing roof tiles that include invisible solar cells. They are made of glass, but from the ground, they look just like regular shingles. So far, the idea is still at the testing stage, with Tesla aiming to overcome the challenges of miniaturizing PV panels down to the size of a single shingle, while keeping costs down. But it could become a solution for people who dislike the look of PV panels.

Keeping It Flexible

Innovators in the industry have been working to create solar technology that is more flexible. Thin-film silicon PV panels are a thin, flexible layer that can be shaped for many uses. It can be attached to another material, such as metal, plastic, or glass, that allows it to be used on the outsides of buildings, including windows. This can greatly increase the building's ability to generate solar power. These thin film layers weigh less than standard PV panels, and they cost less to produce, too. Another advantage is that they work better in cloudy conditions than traditional panels do.

The disadvantages of thin-film silicon PV panels are they are less efficient at turning the energy in sunlight into power. A larger area of a building must also be covered to generate the same amount of electricity. Thin-film silicon PV panels don't last as long, and must be replaced more often.

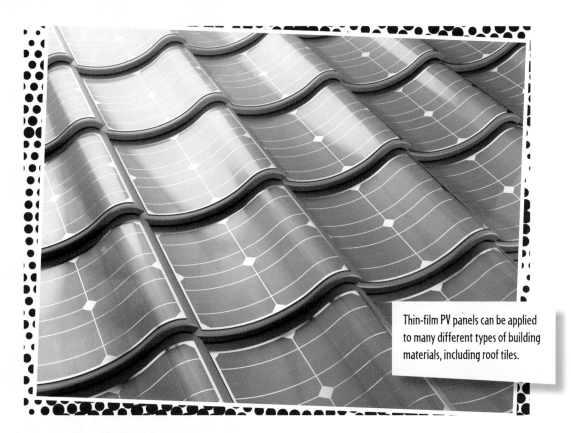

Thin-film PV panels can be applied to many different types of building materials, including roof tiles.

Riding on a Wave

Although the cost of producing solar power fell by around 85 percent between 2009 and 2017, the challenge remains for solar power to meet our growing energy needs. We need solar panels to be more efficient at extracting more of the energy in sunlight. One exciting recent discovery is delivering on that.

Energy Waves

A mineral that is in plentiful supply around the world is emerging as the leader in the race for better PV materials. It is called perovskite. In sunlight, perovskite behaves differently from silicon. All light energy takes the form of waves, and different types of light have different wavelengths. Perovskite captures energy from a different part of the wavelength of sunlight than silicon does. Researchers have found that this makes it better at converting the light energy into power. A typical silicon solar cell converts 21 to 22 percent of sunlight into energy. With perovskite, that could rise to 25 percent.

In 2018, Professor Henry Snaith and his team used perovskite solar cells to break the record, extracting 27.3 percent of the energy in sunlight. What is more, they think there is further room for improvement and that the technology has the potential to reach 33 percent.

The use of perovskite is an exciting development in the use of solar power as a low-cost, renewable source of energy.

These perovskite solar cells are being tested by researchers.

Shifting Solar Solutions

Perovskite can be used in a different way than silicon, too. It does not have to be made into rigid PV panels. Instead, it can be used to make a thin-film solar coating, which can be put on large rolls and used to cover wide areas. It could be built into the fabric of new buildings, in the walls and as windows, because it can be made semitransparent, or partly see-through. Silicon is too heavy to be used in that way.

The potential for perovskite is huge, and it is a hot topic at the moment. Experts think that silicon will probably remain the top choice for large-scale solar farms, while perovskite will be the new choice for smaller spaces, such as homes.

BIG Issues
Solar in Space?

Silicon PV panels have traditionally been used to power **satellites** and other space craft, but transporting these heavy panels into space is expensive and difficult. Using perovskite PV panels in space would be an ideal solution, because it is lighter than silicon and more efficient at creating power from sunlight.

CHAPTER 6

Solar Power Today

Solar power is spreading across the globe. The costs of installing it, for homeowners and for the companies setting up solar power plants, have come down a lot. This has made it a good option for consumers wanting to tap into cleaner energy. Experts think that the amount of installed PV power capacity in the world will have tripled between 2017 and 2023.

Germany was one of the first countries to develop solar power. These panels run alongside the country's highways.

Around the World

China is generating the same amount of solar power as the three next-largest countries put together: Japan, Germany, and the United States. Developing countries, such as India, are investing, or putting money into, the industry. As it becomes clear that large solar power plants can generate an enormous amount of electricity, big companies such as Shell and BP have entered the solar power industry, investing in companies supporting the move toward to bigger and better solar power. Shell is even building its own solar power plant in the Netherlands, with 50,000 panels that will deliver power directly to its own nearby factory.

In Europe, Germany has led the way in solar power over the past 10 years, but other countries are joining in. Wind power has seen more growth, but as the price of solar power falls and becomes more competitive, companies realize that a combination of the two energy sources can provide a more reliable electricity supply. The EU is committed to renewable energy. In 2018, it presented a plan called A Clean Planet for All. The plan included investing in new energy research and technology. It also focused on helping people play their part in creating a cleaner-energy world.

Helping People Use Solar Power

To encourage people to use solar power, some governments have been offering consumers financial benefits, such as paying them for the leftover electricity they have generated and fed into the grid. This is called a feed-in tariff. In several countries, this system of offering feed-in tariffs is coming to an end. If consumers generate surplus electricity, they will have to give it to the grid for free. This is making consumers even more anxious to install a good battery in their home, which will store the leftover electricity for their own use. This is driving the industry to create more affordable, efficient batteries for home use, so consumers can manage their own power.

The old and the new: These solar panels are installed alongside a power plant that burns fossil fuels.

Solar Power in Transportation

With around 7 billion people living on the planet, many millions of us are on the move at any one time. Transportation is the largest and fastest-growing source of greenhouse gas emissions in many countries. The solar power industry has a role to play in helping solve this very serious problem.

Going Electric

One of the biggest areas of innovation in transportation is electric vehicles. Electric vehicles use batteries to store their power. They are charged using the grid, so that if electricity comes from burning fossil fuels, the pollution continues. Solar power in the grid can help keep the whole cycle clean, but there is another, even more direct way that it can be used. The car giant Ford has produced a trial car with solar panels on the roof, which make electricity as the car drives. Other innovators are working on this idea, too. A team of German engineers is developing their solar-powered car, which they call Sion. It has solar cells on the roof, sides, rear, and hood.

Sion is a solar-powered electric car developed by a team of German engineers who want to see an end to the pollution from transportation.

The battery can run the car for 155 miles (250 km) once it has been charged at the grid, but the solar panels can add up to 19 miles (30 km) extra range per day. The Sion is in development, but the company has thousands of orders for it already.

On the Water

Solar-powered boats, though, are on the water right now. The Yacht Club of Monaco, in southern Europe, is usually filled with the luxurious yachts of the wealthy. However, it has created an event to encourage innovators in solar-powered motorboats. Every year, these creative engineers come together to race their boats around the seas off the coast of Monaco, in Europe.

BIG Issues
Solar Power for Planes

Aviation, or the airline industry, contributes up to 10 percent of all harmful greenhouse gases, because the powerful engines that get airplanes off the ground burn so much fuel. The Solar Impulse Foundation believes that we can use solar power for our planes instead. Two pilots in Switzerland, Bertrand Piccard and Andre Borschberg, had a vision for a solar plane that could fly all the way around the world, day and night, without fuel. And they made it happen. The Solar Impulse remained airborne for longer than any aircraft in history, more than five days and five nights. Over the total around-the-world trip, it flew 24,855 miles (40,000 km) without a drop of fuel.

Designers of solar-powered motorboats race their boats against each other to push this technology to the limit.

A Solar-Powered World

Solar power is playing an increasing part in our energy supply today. Around the world, governments, researchers, and businesses are working hard toward taking it even further, so that we can use this endless, free resource to give us the clean energy we so urgently need.

New Energy for the Middle East

Countries in the Middle East have a lot of sunshine, as well as a lot of oil. In the city of Dubai in the United Arab Emirates (UAE), the Mohammed bin Rashid Al Maktoum Solar Park will be one of the biggest in the world when it is completed in 2030, with 2.3 million solar panels spread across an area the size of 800 soccer fields. It will use both PV panels and CSP to provide clean energy to the people of Dubai.

Some countries of the Middle East, such as the UAE, are using their sunshine to generate electricity. Dubai wants to get one-quarter of all its energy from solar power within the next 30 years.

Floating Solar Power

Floatovoltaics, or floating solar power, is another growth area today. In the Brazilian Amazon, for example, about 900 miles (1,448 km) of rain forest were flooded several decades ago for a hydroelectric power plant. It was never as successful as intended. But now, a new floating solar installation is planned for the area to produce enough electricity for about 540,000 Brazilian homes. On a smaller scale, in parts of California, sewage treatment ponds are now being equipped with floating solar panels, and several lakes have been chosen to have solar panels, too. That has a smaller impact on the environment than huge solar power arrays covering miles of the desert, and it also prevents the precious water from evaporating in the heat.

Wearing the Sun's Energy

The latest inventions are making it possible to use solar power in ways we never thought possible. The invention of solar thermal fuel in solid form, which holds heat from the sun and can release it given a trigger, is an exciting development. As well as including this material in car windshields, it could be used to make clothing. Imagine if your clothes could, on demand, release enough heat to keep you warm! We could turn down the heating at home and at work, reducing our consumption of electricity and gas. Some designers are working on solar-powered sunglasses, jewelry, watches, and backpacks, too, to give us power on the go.

Water reservoirs can be used for floating solar panels in heavily built-up areas. The panels also prevent the water from evaporating.

Evolutions of the Future

Energy experts think that the world will add the equivalent of 70,000 new solar panels every hour over the next five years. That is enough to cover 1,000 soccer fields every day. This will change all of our lives for the better.

A Window to the Future

One of the most exciting areas of the future is solar-powered windows. If every building could use its windows to generate electricity, it would forever change the amount of energy we could get from solar power. Every building could be a mini power plant. The science is tricky. It involves using not silicon or perovskite, but tiny particles called quantum dots, which can conduct electricity, or allow it to flow. They are included in a transparent material that is put over the window glass. When the sunshine hits them, they concentrate its energy. Researchers at Los Alamos National Laboratory in New Mexico is developing double-pane windows that can even create shade as well as electricity.

One day soon, all the windows of a city's skyscrapers will be able to generate electricity.

We cannot see infrared waves, but they are in sunlight and their energy could be captured using solar panels.

BIG Issues
The Light We Cannot See

Scientists call the light we can see, including all the colors, the visible spectrum. That is only a small part of the whole range of **electromagnetic waves**, which is what light is made of. Beyond one end of the visible range is ultraviolet (UV) light (which gives us sunburn), and beyond the other end, infrared. We cannot see these with our eyes, but we can use them. For example, we use infrared waves to change television channels using the remote control. Energy scientists are now researching whether it is possible to use solar panels to capture some of the infrared waves in sunlight. The panels would be made using different metals, such as titanium and vanadium. This would give us even more of the energy in sunshine.

Doubling Up

Another invention for the future is solar power that uses photovoltaics and thermal solar power at the same time. When a PV panel generates electricity, it also creates heat. Until now, that heat has been lost to the surrounding air. This new technology, called solar thermophotovoltaics (STPV), captures some of that heat energy and uses it to make the panel generate even more electricity. The research team at MIT has added a new layer to a solar cell's structure that absorbs this heat and converts it to light. This light is then reflected off another solar cell, which uses it to make electricity in the normal way. Scientists think this could allow the cells to extract up to 80 percent of the energy in the sunlight (the current record is less than 30 percent). So far, these innovations have only been created in the lab, but they have huge potential as part of our solar future.

Glossary

alternating current (AC) the type of electricity used to power homes and businesses, and reverses direction quickly and often

array an ordered series or arrangement

atmosphere the blanket of gases around Earth

biomass plant matter used as a source of energy

clean energy energy that does not pollute the environment

climate the regular weather conditions of an area

climate change the changes in climate around the world caused by the gradual increase in the air temperature

commercial power plant a facility the generates large amounts of electricity to sell to the public

consumers people who buy goods and services

direct current (DC) an electric current that only flows in one direction

drought a long, dry period without rain

efficient able to achieve maximum productivity with minimum wasted effort or expense

electric charge electrical energy in something that can be used

electromagnetic waves waves of energy associated with electric and magnetic fields

emissions something, usually harmful, that is put into the air

environment the natural world

evaporates changes from a liquid into a gas

fossil fuels energy sources in the ground, such as coal, oil, and gas, that are limited in quantity

generate to make

generator a machine that converts energy into electricity

geothermal relates to energy harnessed from the heat within Earth

greenhouse gas a harmful gas, such as carbon dioxide, that collects in Earth's atmosphere and traps the heat of the sun

grid the network that distributes electricity from power plants to consumers

hydroelectric using the energy in moving water to produce electricity

innovators people who have smart new ideas about how to do things

installation something that is put in place

manufacturing making

natural disaster a natural event, such as an earthquake, that causes great damage and/or loss of life

nonrenewable will eventually run out

off-grid not using or depending on public utilities, especially the supply of electricity

particles tiny pieces

pollutes makes dirty or adds harmful substances to it

power outages times when the power supply is cut off

power plants places where energy is created

reflective capable of throwing back light or other radiation without absorbing it

renewable describes energy created from sources that do not run out, such as light from the sun, wind, water, and the heat within Earth

reservoirs large human-made areas that contain water

resource something, such as solar power, that is available for use by people

rural related to the countryside

satellites human-made devices that are put into space to orbit, or circle Earth, and send back information

sensors devices that detect something

solar cells tiny structures that convert sunlight into electricity

sustainable able to protect the environment by not using nonrenewable natural resources

thermal related to heat

turbines machines used to convert the movement of air or a liquid into electricity

vaccinate to give an injection that protects against a disease

Find Out More

Books

Burgan, Michael. *The Department of Energy: A Look Behind the Scenes* (U.S. Government Behind the Scenes). Compass Point Books, 2019.

Drummond, Allan. *Solar Story: How One Community Lives Alongside the World's Biggest Solar Plant*. Farrar Straus Giroux, 2020.

Kenney, Karen Latchana. *Solar Energy* (Energy Revolution). Capstone Press, 2019.

Lachner, Elizabeth. *Solar Power* (Exploring Energy Technology). Britannica Educational Publishing, 2019.

Websites

Alliant Energy has a website especially for younger readers at:
www.alliantenergykids.com/RenewableEnergy/SolarEnergy

Ducksters has links to renewable energy sources, including solar power, at:
www.ducksters.com/science/environment/solar_power.php

For more information about solar energy, log on at:
www.eia.gov/energyexplained/index.php?page=solar_home

There is a lot of information on solar power at:
www.funkidslive.com/learn/energy-sources/solar-power-energy-source-fact-file-2

Publisher's note to educators and parents:
All the websites featured above have been carefully reviewed to ensure that they are suitable for students. However, many websites change often, and we cannot guarantee that a site's future contents will continue to meet our high standards of educational value. Please be advised that students should be closely monitored whenever they access the Internet.

Index

About the Author

Robyn Hardyman has written hundreds of children's information books on just about every subject, including science, history, geography, and math. In writing this book she has learned even more about science and discovered that innovation is the key to our future.